about

a coming-of-age poetry anthology

EDITED BY JILL OCONE

Featuring poems by:

John Atholl

Virginia Bach Folger

Jessica Barksdale

Cynthia Bernard

B.A. Brittingham

Jessaca Caset

Joshua Colenda

Cat Dixon

Carol Edwards

Jeremy Gadd

Chris "The Poetic Genius" Green

Benjamin S. Grossberg

Mark Andrew Heathcote

Erin Jamieson

Natalie Kimbell

Payton Kohan

D.L. Lang

Bianca Lopez

Nancy Lubarsky

Fhen M.

J.S. Mannino

Bruce McRae

Norman Minnick

Abigail Ottley

Julia M. Paul

Faith Paulsen

Lois Perch Villemaire

Thomas Rions-Maehren

Stephanie Robertazzi

Brittany Roston and William Roston

Andy Stephen

JC Sulzenko

Jelena Tutnjevic

Henry Vinicio Valerio Madriz

Barry Vitcov

Suellen Wedmore

Andrena Zawinski

Library of Congress Control Number: 2024901257

ISBN

Digital 978-1-63777-535-6

Softcover 978-1-63777-536-3

Published by Red Penguin Books

Bellerose Village, New York

CONTENTS

INTRODUCTION

Welcome to *About Time: A Coming-of-Age Poetry Anthology,* a poetry collection that explores the intricate and elusive tapestry of time weaved by the threads of moments and memories shaped by our experiences and emotions.

Each time we complete another revolution around the sun, we mark our milestone with balloons and cake, but in reality, that milestone is just a speck of insignificance in our planet's 4.5-plus billion years of existence.

None of it matters, yet all of it matters.

We concurrently celebrate and grieve this omnipresent yet invisible entity of time as it is a teacher and a liar, a sage and a fool, an instigator and a rebel. Our lives, our loves, our losses, and our hopes lead each of us to experience time through eerily similar yet vastly different ways.

Time, however, remains a thief on the run. It steals away our days, months, years, and decades in the blink of an eye, but never gets caught or serves any "time" for its crimes. It holds us hostage while simultaneously setting us free, especially in those moments of bliss when we get completely lost in whatever it is we are doing and hours race by like clouds in the gusts high above us.

Time is a gift, the most precious commodity that can be spent but never bought, and most of us callously waste it without savoring or appreciating it.

The poems selected for *About Time: A Coming-of-Age Poetry Anthology* will take you on a fascinating journey through the intricacies of human emotions forged by time. From the simple ticking of a clock's hand to the pivotal moments that alter the course of our destiny, the essence of time found within these collected works capture quiet whispers from the past, the vibrant heartbeat of the present, and unspoken dreams for the future.

Whether it's a bittersweet longing for bygone moments or anticipation for what's to come, the words penned by these poets resonate with the universal rhythms of time that connect us all.

Cozy up and get lost in *About Time: A Coming-of-Age Poetry Anthology* for all time.

Jill Ocone

LIKE NOTHING ENDS

John Atholl

now tell me how all repetition rends
a mind from dwelling dwelling here and now
all days, all loves, all act like nothing ends

i had a lovely lover we were friends
our show is done, we snatch a tardy bow
to show you how all repetition rends

what feeble friends we were just passing trends
whose bond could not outlive vain passion's wow
all days, all loves, all act like nothing ends

at back of clock hide words your mother sends
in love with love she warns still seeking how
to teach us that all repetition rends

sad clock hid more than words for all time tends
to etch in lines deep branded on a brow
all days, all loves, all act like nothing ends

but hopeful hearts will cling, a moment mends
until time triggers one decisive row
now tell me how all repetition rends
all days, all loves, all act like nothing ends

What She Left Behind

Virginia Bach Folger

I remember she would say
ladies wear white gloves
to go into the city. No one
does that anymore, except perhaps
in old black and white movies. In her
dresser drawer I found a pair
of short white cotton gloves, delicate,
with eyelet cutwork on the hems.
Pristine, probably unused. And below them
a soft cashmere pair, palest turquoise,
still in the same white Lord & Taylor box
with its signature long-stemmed rose
that waited under her tree one Christmas.
I don't remember her ever wearing them,
though I had chosen them carefully,
for their softness, for her favorite hue.
Perhaps there was something about
them she hadn't liked, or maybe
she was saving them for a special
occasion, or as she would say, *for good.*

FILE NOT FOUND

Jessica Barksdale

Arriving in triplicate, please note this large package, labeled with date and time,
the when and where everything went wrong, and what we mean by that is the locale
and era, moment, second where you irrevocably became who you are.
Associated friends and family and happenstance bystander accounts are transcribed,
as are (when available) notes from various authorities and institutions.
A description of the effects on you stemming from this incident or situation
are explicated, a clear column of all your former and current despairs.
Some receivers will find home movie archival footage to support yearly,
monthly, daily claims of "It's all your fault" and "I always blamed you." Finally,
you will be able to point clear fingers at the ones who did you wrong.
If possible and if surveillance was granted, audio footage cassettes
are included. Hear the words that blast every day in your head but now
in the awful original. Polaroids will arrive under separate post. Postage due
depending on location. Please do not contact this office again. We've had enough
of your pleading and whining. After obsessing over the above package,
we encourage—nay, we insist—you let this go. Put it down. Bury
or, better yet, burn all the above. Dance around the fire, naked, writhing,
gyrating to the gods that helped you live through it all. Sing to the heavens,
to the earth, to the skies, trees, and creatures. Sing to the bees, vegetables,
and birds on the wing. Wipe your brow, kiss the living person next to you.
Forgive them, those who did not save you. Forgive your wounds, great
and small. Finally, finally, forgive yourself for not forgiving.

Unofficial Time

Cynthia Bernard

My morning hair, before the brush,
is tangled and tinseled
like a dried-out Tannenbaum
tossed on the curb in the middle of January,
and somehow the uninvited frosting
is particularly visible
in the up-too-early hours before dawn.

I can go to a hairdresser for redemption,
or do it myself in the laundry room sink,
but I cannot wash away
those also uninvited times
that have emerged along with the silver
when I can't find the portal back to sleep
even though the world is dark
and, as I brew some tea,
a foghorn serenades me,
penetrating the silence
of my night-time kitchen.

But then again
these are the times
when gestating poems whisper to me,
asking to be written,
when I gaze at a waning crescent of moon
and catch my first glimpse
of the blushing morning sky,
when I watch the fog as it curtseys to the ocean
and slowly dances away,
when What's True and I can sit and chat,
undefended,

laugh and cry together,
and make up after yesterday's squabble,
and when, in those last few moments
before I greet my sweetheart
and officially begin the day,
I sit with the foghorn and my aliveness,
gifted by my tinsel
with such a lovely Now,
much more precious than sleep.

BADLANDS

B.A. Brittingham

What is this surface suggestive of short
hills and gorges? Flesh colored, it calls to mind
the buttes and plateaus of high desert country.
Mako Sica, that's what it resembles! 'Badlands'
as the Sioux called that collection of unique
mesas and mounts on their South Dakota rez.

There is a blue line running through it —
a river or a temporary arroyo? Water is a
singular commodity here; too much and the
ravines grow deeper. Those darkened areas
may resemble sun-scorched rocks but they
are markings of another, archaic kind.

Now I must smile at my own folly, for
this all is just time making merry with me:
the flattened mountains are the once smooth
skin that was mine long ago. The azure track
is but a protruding vein marking the wasteland
of an arm seven decades old. The rocks are
no more than the freckles of senior skin.

But they announce that here lives long life —
However much strewn with wonder or strife.

QUEEN ANNE'S LACE

Jessaca Caset

Queen Anne's Lace
Was a wildflower that appeared
At the end of my street near a bench
Where you caught the 166 to New York.
Regarded as weed and nothing more,
It returned... every year, over and over
Despite the humid northeast summers
And winters dressed in hoar frost
Reminiscent of a noir film,
All platinum blonde and sequins,
Hard cold in the passing headlights.
The soil where it grew was also
The only patch of earth exposed
Powdery grey, it scarcely concealed
Wind blown amongst its roots
The odd crumpled candy wrapper,
Cigarette butt, or occasional coffee cup.
My grandmother called them lace caps,
The same name she gave her lace
Tatting, intricate hand woven knots
Connected by the thinnest of thread,
Weighted around the circular edges
With multicolored beads purchased
In little packets from the dollar store.
Her tatting did resemble that flower too;
Blossoming in an outward spiral form
Draped over glasses of sweet tea
To discourage the random fly or bee
From drowning itself in a sugary sea
While together we would sit sweating,
Aluminum folding chairs of woven nylon

Tucked in the shade of our building;
Our gaze drifting up above our heads,
August heat a shimmering veil beyond,
Coveting the air conditioner hanging
Cantilevered from the window
Of our neighbor four flights above;
Mechanical hum and condensate,
Rhythmically dripping to form
A wet stain on the concrete.
Lace caps and lace tatting,
Both the color or aged paper,
Hers tipped in rainbow hues.

MAUSOLEUM

Joshua Colenda

I walked along this busy road,
To finally find at the end,
My tomb.
I'll fill it full of lots of things,
So it my life will prove.

I'll fill it with my thoughts and deeds,
My schemes,
And dreams,
And memories.
Every thread of my tapestry,
I'll even bring the loom.

I'll carve my name in runes of stone,
And write of every seed I've sown,
And every road I've roamed.
Passersby will read the walls, shake their heads, and say,
"I wish I could have met this man,
But he was working on his grave.
Just down the road,
There is a shrine,
To a girl,
Who always found the time,
To talk to you,
When she was alive,
Surely it was she,
Who left this world too soon."

The Show

Cat Dixon

act i
all your questions will be answered
by the set designer who will fire
23 shots straight to your heart

act ii
you're ageless, famous, patient
precariously balanced on a flask
filled with water from the river

act iii
on the sketchpad you draw
fin and feather, you list the scenes
that will complement the map, the monster

act iv
your role is peacemaker tottering
in little circles on a stool, fully
exposed, saggy, ready for the interview

act v
you talk to hear yourself talk
you want to feel something
the ice stings those sunset stars

act vi
all your layers are removed by force
all your words are in cages
you can't put the drink back in the bottle

REALITY (UN)RESOLVED

Carol Edwards

Aging somehow catches us by surprise;
every morning we see our mirror faces
"Yes, that's what I look like now,"
yet when confronted
with etchings of a before-likeness
we feel cheated, cry "Thief!"
though we see these same designs
in our parents' skin, children's –
lines the same roads on the same maps;

with ears covered and voices loud
we drown out the engine sound
while dark windows
mirror the tunnel ahead,
we the Schrodinger's cat
cowered in this poison box
simultaneously alive and dead –
maybe we won't have to find out
if we keep the lid closed tight.

November Lilies

Jeremy Gadd

November lilies were nodding in the breeze
like casual acquaintances passing when
a friend called to say a mutual friend had died.
Did I want to know the details of her death?
And I thought, we die in increments, by gasps
or by sudden demise but I would rather know
more about how she lived, her idiosyncrasies;
her irrepressible *joie de vivre,* for it is the
living entity who will always occupy my heart
and death will find us impossible to part.
We humans are individually distinctive, unique;
sometimes attractive in body and mind
and sometimes not or unkind but, even after
mortality, there is only human inter-connectivity.

GRANDMA'S HOUSE

Chris "The Poetic Genius" Green

I can hear the call from Grandma's Kitchen
Beckoning me for fried chicken,
Can hear her voice coming down the lane
Memory toying with my brain
Knowing the house is vacant now.

I can see my pop waving to me from my steps.
I'm wishing I knew how much time we had left
In those days,
Those days, the house was a Sunday dinner away from paradise,
Love filled every room, and soul food filled every belly.
That house was small, but fit every individual family,
A beautiful collection of all we are.
Me and my cousins filling the yard with distractions from grown talk
Playing kickball hoping not to hit a window,
Pop chasing us down the lane with his voice when we do,
Playing hide and seek or riding bikes,
The invisible barrier in front of the street,
Getting to the edge we weren't allowed to cross...

My grief telling me I'm on the edge of memories I shouldn't cross.

I miss them, how they were relics and glue
Pointed to a time long before me, but held us together.
Now they're still together, but gone.
Mother's home our new gathering place,
Sitting at the grown folks table my uncle in Pop's seat,
My aunt in Grandma's,
And their names ringing through conversation,
like legends.

Hard to find acceptance, hard to agree to the terms,
They had a contact to keep with God,
How I never knew they were approaching the deadline,
How my family is so close
To another memory I'll have to fold up and tuck away in my mind
For safe keeping,
Hoping it's never vacant
As Grandma's house.

THE ARROGANCES

Benjamin S. Grossberg

I had the arrogance of takes no pills.
I had all the arrogances. The arrogance
of waiting for better. Of refusing
to explain. Of no gray in my beard
after forty and none on my chest,
which I flaunted on various apps.
I do not mention the arrogance of
regular dentistry and a reliable car.
But I had those, too. I never had that
of height or I-can-beat-you-up, useful
both for erotic and commercial
applications, but I still found ways
to get along, mostly by staying in corners
and wearing boots. Death's arrogance
flummoxed me, its supercilious refusal
of even the most supplicant address.
My mother, for example, when my father
drives up to her grave, conveniently
located at the end of a row. Does
the nearby tree explain her hauteur?
Not every plot has one. In winter,
he parks beneath it, engine on, heat
going, staying as long as he can take it.
My arrogance on the phone as he
tells me this manifests in platitudes.
I won't get started on the arrogance
of platitudes. Enough to say that I
was full of it—like stones in my pocket,
weighing me into a lake. But other
arrogances buoyed me. Looks-good
-for-his-age, especially, which,

in my arrogance, I took as an insult.
And hope as expectation, and hell no
to the obvious. But pills every morning
should have been my first clue.
And increasing blotchiness of face.
And that rafter of men not texting back.
One by one, the departing arrogances:
little ballerinas twirling off stage, each
in its puffed-out skirt. The arrogance
of consciousness may well be last to go,
the final ballerina, pirouetting away.
And look, her slipper's come loose!

LIFE IS THE BOOKMARK BEFORE A PASSAGE OF SLEEP

Mark Andrew Heathcote

There are passages in life
No one should have to reread.
Rooms within a sprawling maze
only we should unadvisedly revisit,
Even only then in whispered retreating footsteps.
We all haunt a past that has no objectivity
other than to leave us alone, abandoned
with ever-worsening, superimposed regrets.
Life is the bookmark before a passage of sleep
where the leafing forefinger can discover
a new ever-changing character, a charioteer
leading the course, the pack and hasn't the time
or the inclination to look back for fear
of veering off track. It is here
We discover our true purpose and meaning
and not just a face, an empty reflection
in the primordial mirror of nothingness.
Here, we find our true selves,
ever-present and begrudgingly at times forgiving.

IT'S TIME TO GO

Erin Jamieson

I bathe in shadows,
ashes fusing to my veins
—cavernous dusk erupts
& I cannot tell crimson
from velvety black nor
how I became this haunted
being that inhibits your
lonely rooms-rooms
you invite your new lover.

After the funeral you told
anyone who would listen:
no more reservations just
microwave spaghetti congealing
to now-forgotten plates.

Once, you look away
from your lover
open a window

As if to tell me
It's time to go.

AND WE DREAM

Natalie Kimbell

the illusion of forever
up in the starred night's sky
releasing our dust in the hourglass
shooting stars against ebony

Up in the starred night sky
we dream of endless tomorrows
shooting stars against ebony
searching heaven's flowing folds

We dream of endless tomorrows
we plan as if time was friend
searching heaven's flowing folds
as we cascade from sight

We plan as if time was friend
and we dream the illusion of forever
as we cascade from sight
releasing our dust in the hourglass

THREE DAYS

Payton Kohan

The First Day was of pain
Sharp,
As a blade upon the skin
And of a choice –
Of all she could offer
Only to bear
Her heart on her sleeve
And to place her trust
In Three days,
The hours – sand
In an hourglass,
And in the hope
That it was enough

On the Second Day she wondered,
Did he love her too?
How do you measure a life in time?
How do you guide the course of love?
How do you weigh
The Worth
Of an immortal soul?

On the Third Day she knew the cost
Of a Choice
Of Pain
Of Love and Life.
She understood the length of Time,
And how short and unfair
It could be

Her legs gave out,

Her lungs as light as the foam
And her voice no longer carried
Across the ocean breeze
The sun rose behind the horizon,
And somehow –
Time
Began to slow

Until suddenly
Three days
Became Three Hundred years,
A future as bright
As the morning sun,
As tangible as the waves,
As unbound as the salty air –
With a promise
Greater than time

And only Eternity
To follow.

DESIRES OF A NEW AGE

D.L. Lang

I was born into a country divided
by barbed wire, walls, and war.
Shuffled around this one
not of my own accord.

Nearing forty now,
I long to be as steady
as an ancient tree,
rising above history.

The trees sway softly,
dancing branches kiss,
as the goldfinches chant
their morning prayers.

The tea kettle whistles,
steam slowly rising,
like a freight train
en route to the coast.

My bare feet are grateful
for the softness of the rug
as it hugs my toes
with its labyrinth of floral.

I watch the illusion of peace
fade softly into the newsprint,
morphing into an unpredictable
timeline of current events.

Searching for stability,

perhaps, my teacup
is something I can hold onto—
something reliable
in this hurricane of headlines.

The world grows smaller
with every passing moment.
A cocktail of aging and pain
comes the somber realization:

There is as much safety now
in solitude as there is in numbers
when reality has become negotiable.

I long to pull a J.D. Salinger,
escape into sweet anonymity,
and be embraced by the forest,
living among flocks of birds
who know no such thing as fame.

In the Dissonance of Time

Bianca Lopez

To seek great fortitude
One must not wither with time,
For time is of the essence
Resist it only to acquiesce it.

For who is this bearer of time?
Walking solo, forlorn an unfamiliar paradigm;
One must refrain from thoughtless years misbegotten
And what gives if the memories rotten?

Sadness in virtue is all that seems
In trials and tribulations thought a heavy stream.
Willpower besought, desperately inane
Wither yonder, hope is the force contained.

A split of a second, a fraction of an eye,
When the storms circumference peaks at dawn-
So shall one remain, kept in dissonance of thoughts
So that when our hearts shatter and the pieces strewn
The mind collects the parts to brave its many moons.

Fear not dear time, as time is on the move!
Do as one pleases, oh fear! the guise of successes only ally.
In the dissonance of time, the ones who seek shall find
Not all is lost when loss is time.

STONEHENGE

Nancy Lubarsky

As if time and the
sun could be
harnessed, held
back by huge,
heavy stones,
carved and
balanced with
bones and antlers,
dragged and pulled
in a circle, placed
there by the ancients,
millennium before
metal and machines.
Today's calendars
are soft pages,
digital pulses—light
and fleeting. Now time
travels at high speeds
away from us.
It's captured in gray
hairs, frail bones
and friends passing.

OUTSIDE THE BLOCK UNIVERSE

Fhen M.

Your bronze-colored hair swayed,
physique like a Greek marble statue
walked along a street of cobblestone
across a well-painted pavilion
and followed me as I was about to go home.

I walked swiftly
knowing that you were behind me
as if you wanted a conversation
maybe to talk about law, love, or marriage
you do not quite understand.

As I was noticing you
my pace slowed down...

Oh time past, I may only perceive you
outside the block universe
like a ghost who doesn't care of the living
a picture that doesn't mind my gaze
an information that can't be destroyed.

There is no way of going back
to offer her ice cream or chocolate,
to invite her to drink a cup of coffee,
anything and everything
as long as she is with me
or I am with her.

Past is real, memory is real
imagination is real?
maybe to the heart of a man who loves.

Ephemera

J.S. Mannino

Somewhere, somehow, someway everything changed.
I stopped being the sun and the moon
And became the just bearable goof
Good for a few laughs every now and then
No heavy lifting, just the light stuff
And in a blink, it all passed...

Somewhere along the way
I stopped being essential
They stopped needing or I stopped being needed
A bath in the sink became a protest in the streets
A few wobbly steps, a thousand-mile road trip
And in a blink, they evolved...

Somehow, they grew
No longer dependent on my wisdom
And swelling with defiance
In asking, they questioned, they grew
Overcoming my antiquated notions
They transcended my philosophies
And in a blink, they were me...

Someway time burgeoned
After all, they are only small for a minute
And before too long, I became a footnote
*Non-essential reference material
Like a tattered and torn thesaurus at the bottom of a drawer
Sentimentality keeps it around
But no one remembers why they ever needed it
And in a blink, all the dust settled...

Somewhere along the way
My status as "god" was downgraded
First to minor deity
To necessary evil
To whatever state I currently occupy
Anachronistic relic?
Historical Cleric?
Goofball the Graybeard?
And in a blink, the ink on my id dried…

Somehow impossibly
Everything happened all at once
I know, I know…I get it
Kids grow
Time flows
Circumstances change
Everything starts anew
But did it have to pass so quickly?
Did the "moment of remembering"
Have to become the "recently forgotten"?
Don't blink cause you'll miss it all…

Someway I survive
Of all the lives I've known
Of all the titles I've worn
This one has been my favorite
So perhaps now I must concede
Step carefully down with nothing left to say
But the title I once stylishly wore
Has now been handed down
To the three lives, I delicately wrought
The once proud Daddy
Answering now to "Dad."
Dares to blink

How Sunday Was

Bruce McRae

Mondays' child had gone a-whoring.
Tuesday lorded it over the counter-tops.
Wednesday was whining.

On the first day God created himself.
Time rioted.
Light bent over to look at a shoe.
The worst day in living memory,
and the five-and-dime planets were humming.
Sunset wept over love lost.
Stars burnt through the blankets of heaven.
The third day, and God spoke:
"Let there be quiet,
so I may contemplate my bafflement."
The fourth day was unaccounted for.

Then a fifth day, supple and pliant.
Lo, from reticular cloudshine
came the voice of rain being humbled.
Our master grumbled,
the Sabbath disheveled and shabby.
Clearing his throat, he drew a line.
He painted the air yellow.

Out of the earth came a very odd flower.

New Horizons

Norman Minnick

The New Horizons space probe is the size
of my parents' four-poster bed

and is speeding away from the earth
at 31,000 miles per hour.

It is almost out of fuel
and cannot slow down.

It has used the gravitational pull of Jupiter
to slingshot deeper into space.

Now it has reached Pluto
near the edge of our solar system.

It will escape our sun's pull
and never return.

Many folks my age and older
would agree that time goes by faster

the older we get. Children are growing
at alarming rates, just as our parents foretold.

I am attending more funerals and taking
copious trips to the bathroom.

The toys I played with as a child
are in museums. Last year's videos

appear grainy and out of sync.
When, I wonder, did I pass Jupiter?

THE BOXER

Abigail Ottley

You go down hard like a frozen side of beef
or a hundredweight sack of potatoes.
Like a man through a trapdoor, falling
like a stone through the dark.

You go down mid-sentence. An hour after
lunch, half in, half out of the kitchen,
your knees buckle and your legs give way.
There's no sound but a grunt of mild surprise.

You are sprawling and winded, we see straight away
there's no possible way we can lift you.
Two frightened women, not young or strong,
one who needs help to get dressed.

We do our best but we know we're beaten.
Knowing it too, you are angry.
Strain your once-beefy arms to heave yourself
back into the light.

A boxer in your day, you have dwindled to this,
an old man's rage wrapped in a blanket.
Paramedics rehearse their professional banter,
haul your bulk upright *on three.*

As they load you up and the big engine purrs.
they tell us you'll be *home in no time.*
Inform us later you *slipped away.*
But we know you went down hard.

CLOUDS DRIFT ENDLESSLY

Julia M. Paul

As a child, I tried to count
to infinity. In the thousands,
I was called in to dinner.
Time hurried on with its countdown.

I know nothing of eternity,
although an egret stood
on the dock this morning
for what seemed like one.
Still as death, except
for its shifting eyes.

When it opened its wings,
lifted its heft and left me,
it was forever.
To leave solid ground
without dread
we living might learn
from our dead.

Before her death,
my elderly mother
called out for her mother.
Proof that a single word
can be a perfect prayer.
There's still time, we said,
as if forever were
an unopened package
left on our front stoop.

THE MIDDLE

Faith Paulsen

Feet a-dangle we skim the canopy
silent traversal our storied leap behind.
Have we lost that once-immunity
foolish trust in the middle of the line?
Sneaking a look at the valley's deep drop
the chance no certainty of grief.
What if one of us should fall – or stop—
On this zipline it is when and not if.
My ragged soul a flag in gale-force winds
everyday anniversaries strung between—
Less distant every year the upward bend
though waterfalls and anthems intervene.
Mid-freefall I choose my center of gravity—
In physics and movement I hold you close to me.

PICTURES OF DAD

Lois Perch Villemaire

1
I stand with Dad
on the beach
where rippled edges
of the ocean run flat
and tiny crabs bubble
into the sand.
He holds my hand,
I wave to the photographer.

I'm missing teeth.
He has a crew cut,
and loves the beach.
We jump the waves.
Hotels along the boardwalk
fade in the distance.

2
I walk with Dad
down the aisle.
We don't speak,
moving like robots,
both nervous, eyes front.
As Dad kisses my cheek
the photographer snaps us.

His hair is salt and pepper.
Mine is long and dark.
Seated smiling faces merge
into the background.
Dad delivers me
into position
for the ceremony.

3
I sit with Dad
holding tight to his hand
as we tell him
Mom passed away.
My heart aches
at the unfamiliar sounds
of his anguish
after 65-years together.

4
I huddle with my siblings
at the service
where words about Dad
are spoken.
Through my tears
I see him in my brothers' eyes.

MY GRANDPA WAS SANTA

Thomas Rions-Maehren

My grandpa was Santa. Really.
Real beard, real belly,
all the other kids were so jealous.

But I was too little to understand the coldness
my dad showed towards ol' St. Nick
and to see the longing under his jolliness
to make things right with the son

whom he rode away from on his motorcycle
so long ago. I was too young to know that,
for every piece of shrapnel left in his arms,
which were so fun to feel, running my tiny fingers
over the raised bumps where bullets hid,

there was another scar
left in his mind. I never could figure out why,
on my trips to Santa's summer home in Arizona –
where I did jackknives off the diving board
into his bottomless pool, the chlorine burning
my eyes – he would seem so restless in the morning
if a helicopter flew over the house in the night. It never
made that much noise. I'd sleep right through it.

And when the years of pills, of crime, of drugs
of running from his memories, of delivering
morbid gifts from an armored sleigh,
finally did what nobody in Vietnam could,
I asked why we weren't going to the funeral. Because,
my dad told me, he never gave
anything to anyone except the box rusted medals
he left behind.

STACCATO SECONDS

Stephanie Robertazzi

The connection between Mother Nature and Father *Time*
happened solely by a game of chance.
The iconic story that would change the course of *time*
and create a void in the space that one didn't know existed.
An emptiness that will eventually fade
creating memories that would last a *lifetime*.

-Strike 1-
From the dawn of *time*, a tree symbolized the deepest blessings…
rooted into one's heart and forever in mind.
A seed that now was planted, a blessing not deserved,
a gift that keeps on giving, and unconditional love.
The mother and her new-born obsession,
a thought that never seems to stop.
Life mimicking the sound of a clock.
Tick, tock. Tick, tock.

-Strike 2-
Heartbeats are a descending series of staccato seconds.
Seconds turn into minutes. Hours into days:
inevitably never stopping from turning into months –
hopefully never making it to years of mourning.
Those years to look back and see from the beginning of *time*,
that this was more than just feelings from the heart.
After all this *time*.
Tick, tock. Tick, tock.

-Strike 3-
Time seemed to move faster when the reel was playing.
Coining the phrase "all the *time* in the world,"
But ironically *time* ran out – no longer the priority.
Gazing at the watch — have we been given the gift of *time*?
No, the clock broke at the strike of 8,
after being convinced that it would last forever ∞
Oh how the *timing* was off.
Tick, tock. Tick, tock.

-Strike 4-
Amazing how *time* flies — was it fun?
A galaxy full of stars, but no more tomorrows.
Ultimately and *untimely* frozen in this moment of *time*.
Forever wanting to flashback to a *time* existing as a memory.
Spare *time* is now non-refundable in the rearview mirror-
confined to the ill-fated grips yanking away the control.
It was only a matter of *time*.
Tick, tock. Tick, tock.

-Strike 5-
Like walking through a minefield or over the shattered eggs –
step by step not knowing what comes next.
Time is at a standstill — is this really it?
It's like a ticking *time*-bomb, just waiting to go off.
One wrong move could change the course of *time*.
Surely the battery of effort could decide.
Time after *time*.
Tick, tock. Tick, tock.

-Strike 6-

But *time* discovers the truth:

Silence isn't empty; it's full of answers.

It knows no laws, takes no pity — *time* for change.

They say "give it *time*" and declare *time* heals all.

Wishing to turn back the hands of *time*

Never wanting to know the feeling of *time* and space…

The essence now in the creation of the bucket list for the empty nest.

Killing *time.*

Tick, tock. Tick, tock.

-Strike 7-

Tomorrow is never promised so how much *time* is left?

As the granules dripped through the hourglass;

Was it written in the sand? Was it washed away,

never existed at all, or a dream that never came true?

Happy *times*, sad *times*, difficult *times.*

Maybe *sometime*, someday, next *time.*

What a *time* that was.

Tick, tock. Tick, tock.

-Strike 8-

Not knowing it was the last *time* until it was –

feeling the force of magnetic influence – out of luck, out of *time.*

Love will transcend the hopes, the maybes, and the what if's.

As beauty fades to ashes, the colors begin to gray.

Certainly this can't be the end, it's only "halfway."

Hopefully in *time* …Only *time* will tell.

Tick, tock. Tick, tock.

THIEF

Brittany Rostron and William John Rostron

We were living lives of passion
Never wanting to go slow
Never thinking, 'bout tomorrow
Never choosing to say no

We had the promise of a dream
To keep our fates at bay
Then, then came the Thief
And took it all away

In time, Time takes everything
No memories to treasure.
How long will he steal from me
This Thief of my forever.

Savage delight at my plight
Smiling as he grimly reaps
His dance brings my denial
His laugh brings my defeat

How could we listen to our hearts
Forgiving all our sins
Now we'll forever be apart
Just a song in the wind

In time, Time takes everything
No memories to treasure.
How long will he steal from me
This Thief of my forever.

Look here, stiff frozen in fear
Of the man I've always been
Fear of what I'll never be
Fear I'll never win

My words are left unspoken
The new dawn brings no sun
In the darkness I lie broken
Silent and undone

In time, Time takes everything
No memories to treasure.
How long will he steal from me
This Thief of my forever
This Thief of my forever.

I Believe in Immortality

Andy Stephen

I believe in immortality
Fate doesn't dictate vitality.

Every butterfly's wing
The melodies we sing
Breed newfound thinking.

Joy was locked inside a tomb
While gravity lingered in the dark corners of my room.
An old friend's bile that I still ingest;
"It seems you want to be depressed.
Happiness is part-choice
Unlock your little joys."

I believe in immortality
Fate doesn't dictate vitality.

When our stomachs spill out
And we lie fetal on the ground,
We crave newfound thinking.

I had a brother
Who found his tomb in the summer.
For a while he had been sick
As he surrendered to a narcotic.
With his death something churned within
As if controlled by an apparition.
My feet attached to strings
That pull toward new beginnings.

I believe in immortality
For even in death
We live on.

Writer's Note: Naloxone (Narcan), the medication that reverses the effects of an opioid overdose, is free at any pharmacy in New Jersey. It is incredibly safe, easy-to-use, and effective. Seek medical attention after using. If you are struggling with addiction call: 1-800-662-4357.

NO SUGAR TODAY

JC Sulzenko

air purifier hiss.
traffic hum.

a wan sky. rooftop rain weeping
into the marrow of the house.

more hours of night than day.
no one to call.

    not mother—morning conversations
    about Seinfeld nothingness,
    or headlines, or the best dark-chocolate
    with Leonard's songs on low.
    she left me her silence at 90.

    not childhood pal—we roamed backyards,
    imagined kingdoms down to contours of sand,
    talked through middle age, survived
    lovers, mourned, celebrated. now we set
    dates to see each other on a small screen.

    not the children. my sweet children
    with their own children. they work,
    they parent from home with no time off.
    i connect, we connect when
    they agree. only then.

i sip my latte.
cold, it tastes of november.

STOP

Jelena Tutnjevic

Pedestrian rain washes away Palladian castles
Old neighborhoods
Complain about new neighborhoods
Old neighbors band together
To chastise the newcomers
It ain't what it used to be.

That parking garage over there, my son,
I worked there
From dawn to dusk
Every day
For twenty years.

Where that parking garage is now
Used to be a park
In my time,
Horses pranced there dragging the carriages with lords and ladies.

You'd never know by the look of that building
That used to be a meat packing plant.
That used to be a club.
That used to be a family restaurant.
There were barely any houses here in my time.

He ain't Fred Astaire
And no truth such as that was ever less important.
The one that came before, unaware of his successor
And the successor in the dark about the one he's judged against.
Patiently waiting for those who know of some better past to die out
and let him claim his spotlight.

At which time
He becomes good old days himself
Living off his old glory
A revered blueprint for everything that comes
Uncomfortably accepting the honor
Of no choice
An overture to perishing.

She brings back the old glamor
Happier past
Simpler times
Eyes closed
In general agreement
To dark attics, alcoves and cellars
As it was oh so good
For most of us.

Old lovers complain of new lovers
Younger, more beautiful, yes,
But have no class, no grace.
And no truth such as that was ever less important.
Because in a new, shiny, gated tower
Away from old lovers' praying eyes
A new chapter has began
New, crispy, fresh,
Bright colors
That cannot phantom the prospect of fading.
And everything that's old is forsaken, and rejected, dismissed and done with.
Nothing of what it was is allowed, revered, nor remembered.

That sweet moment when the new
Foolishly thinks it's never going out of fashion
It never will become sluggish and tired
Same old
And soon enough

Old news and then
Just
Old.

And sooner still
Replaced.

AGES

Henry Vinicio Valerio Madriz

Innocently step by step I timidly go.
From my loving mother's hands to
explore this world that is mine now.
Smiling at the odd winds that blow.

Playfully step by step I curiously go.
From my manly father's guidance to
interaction with the world amazed me.
Looking at an uncertain society's plea.

Challengingly step by step I sure go.
From my beloved family's roots to
conquer this world that shows creeds.
Showing off skills with human greed.

Solidly step by step I consciously go.
From my steady marriage's home to
study this world, with desire and pride.
Collecting memories and tears I cried.

Wisely step by step I peacefully go.
From my own living soul's voice to
fly away from dream to dream and so.
Resting my pace which became slow.

Joy, anger, love, and sorrow have paved the road.

CAR MOONS

Barry Vitcov

Bidding goodnight to all
the objects in his room
after being read *Goodnight Moon,*
he asks over and over
read again, read again.
It's about the age
when he called headlights car moons,
when learning a language
required invention and convention
before halogen, the loss of innocence,
and the insistence of technology.
When making sense of the world
was a game of finding relevance
and personal meaning.
When a moon landing
was still a novelty.
But those cars whizzing towards us
with their twin moons lighting the way
caused giggling and easy joy.
I wish there were more car moons.

A Fisherman's Wife Greets the Dawn Alone

Suellen Wedmore

1820

I was 18 then, believing
in a vast and fertile sea,
when he wooed me

from Dogtown to Harbor—
a man who tasted of salt
and trawled for quicksilver,

scales heaped around his ankles
like coins. Who understood
the power of a nor'east gale,

the loneliness of the trough
between swells. Coffee mug in hand,
I listen now for crash

of surf against granite shore,
the rattle of spindle and lantern,
a schooner run aground.

Last month, my friend's husband
fishing bound, sailed out
and never returned....

2020

I was 18 then, believing
in a vast and fertile sea,
when he wooed me

from stairwell to breakwater—
a man who tasted of sweat, who
was at ease with muscle's might,

the thud of haddock
on a metal deck,
the sea's fickle manners.

The truth is there are many truths:
the dignity of a man
working alone, as well as

the weighing of his toil.
The certainty of catch limits,
fuel costs, whale-friendly gear;

sometimes, in this morning sky
I see what he sees: a loan, past due
in the midst of a nor'east gale....

as the sun rises
I dream baskets of mackerel, hake, and cod,
a calm sea,
a welcoming harbor.

ALGORITHMS OF MEMORIES

Scott Wiggerman

golden shovel based on a Buson haiku

I don't remember what colors came before,
just the dazzling gleam of this watermelon sunset.

I don't remember which warbler sang so brightly,
only which love of many endures and shines.
I don't remember June's heavenly spectacle, but the
blue pulse persists from a single welcoming star.

And I will never forget the enthusiastic caress of a
baby's palm on my grandmother's fingers, withered
grasses, that soft shaft of white on a hard old field.

It is Enough for Now,

Villanelle for Mornings

Andrena Zawinski

It is enough in this first breath of morning
to lie here with you, light slipping between us,
our fingers laced, lids still swollen with sleep.

Enough to listen to the distant sound of the early train,
song of a buoys in the bay, wind bells in the breeze.
It is enough in this first breath of morning

to talk about the night's dreams, and to dream
across seas, up rivers, into the wild hills,
our fingers laced, lids still swollen with sleep.

It is enough to hold onto each other,
to keep each other still and quiet in place.
It is enough in this first breath of morning,

enough to breathe in the sky, the bright of sun
crossing and washing the continents of our bodies.
It is enough in this first breath of morning,
our fingers laced, lids still swollen with sleep.

MEET OUR CONTRIBUTORS

John Atholl

After a serious illness in his mid-forties John Atholl was swept up in a healing flood of words. Since then it has taken nearly twenty years to hone his poetic craft enough to be publishable. John works as a professional oral storyteller and language teacher. He lives near Frankfurt in Germany.

Virginia Bach Folger

Virginia Bach Folger lives in Schenectady, New York. She has a BA from Montclair State University and an MA from Seton Hall University. Ginny has worked as a gas station attendant, paralegal, switchboard operator, claims adjuster and corporate learning and development manager. She has previously published in *Constellations: A Journal of Poetry and Fiction*, *Adanna*, *The Fourth River*, and others.

Jessica Barksdale

Jessica Barksdale's sixteenth novel, *What the Moon Did*, was published February 2023 by Flexible Press. Her short story collection, *Trick of the Porch Light*, was published September 2023. She's published two poetry collections: *When We Almost Drowned* (2019) and *Grim Honey* (2021). She taught at Diablo Valley College in Pleasant Hill, California, and continues to teach for UCLA Extension and in the online MFA program for Southern New Hampshire University. She lives in the Pacific Northwest with her husband.

Cynthia Bernard

Cynthia Bernard is a woman in her early seventies who is finding her voice as a poet and writer of flash fiction and essays after many years of silence. A long-time classroom teacher and a spiritual mentor, she lives and writes on a hill overlooking the ocean, about 25 miles south of San Francisco. Her writing has appeared in more than 55 journals and anthologies in the US and internationally, and she was selected by Western Rivers Conservancy to serve as the Poet-Protector of Deer Creek Falls in the northern Sierra Nevada foothills.

B.A. Brittingham

Born and raised in the grittiness of New York City, Brittingham spent a large segment of her adult years in the blue skies and humidity of South Florida. Today she resides along the magnificent (and sometimes tumultuous) shores of Lake Michigan with its ample opportunities for creative contemplation. The author has published essays in the *Hartford Courant*; short stories in Florida Literary Foundation's hardcover anthology, *Paradise*; in the 1996 Florida First Coast Writers' Festival, in Britain's World Wide Writers. Recently published in *WELL READ* Magazine Aug. 2023 was the essay "Feed the Beast;" followed in Dec. 2023 by "Another View-Judas Season."

Jessaca Caset

Jessaca Caset says: I work in the medical profession but have been a bibliophile since I could first read, and I also like to write…a lot. I believe to read and write is the secret alchemy of the human experience.

Joshua Colenda

Joshua Colenda is a sergeant in the US Army National Guard who lives in Salt Lake City with his two dogs. He enjoys hiking and playing the guitar.

Cat Dixon

Cat Dixon is the author of *What Happens in Nebraska* (Stephen F. Austin University Press, 2022) along with six other poetry chapbooks and collections. She is a poetry editor with *The Good Life Review*. Recent poems published in *The Book of Matches*, *North of Oxford*, *hex*, and *The Southern Quill*.

Carol Edwards

Carol Edwards is a northern California native transplanted to southern Arizona. She grew up reading classic and fantasy novels, climbing trees, and acquiring frequent grass stains. She currently enjoys a coffee addiction and raising her succulent army. Her poetry has been published in myriad anthologies, periodicals, and blogs, including *Space & Time, Uproar, Red Penguin Books, Southern Arizona Press, White Stag Publishing, The Post Grad Journal, Written Tales Magazine, The Wild Word, Black Spot Books,* and *Lit Shark Magazine.* Her debut poetry collection, *The World Eats Love,* released April 2023 from The Ravens Quoth Press. IG @practicallypoetical, Twitter/FB @practicallypoet, www.practicallypoetical.wordpress.com

---

Jeremy Gadd

Jeremy Gadd is an Australian author and poet whose most recent publication was *Driving Into the Dark,* a selection of 60 previously published poems (Ginninderra Press, Adelaide, 2022). He has also published novels, short stories, and had plays produced. He has Master of Arts and PhD degrees from the University of New England.

Chris "The Poetic Genius" Green

Chris Green is a poet from Gloucester, Virginia, writing with the hopes to live up to his moniker "The Poetic Genius." The Poetic Genius recently won the Poetry Society of Virginia's Honoring Fatherhood award with "Breaking Myth" a poem about the misconceptions about black fathers. On July 19th (Juneteenth) he was published by Inlandia for their anthology "These Black Bodies Are..." featuring his poems "Reparations," "Monuments," and "Right to be Black." Sunday, November 19th, his poems "Breaking Myth," "Shovel," "Unbothered," and "Deep Roots/Upon Finding Out My Son Doesn't Like Being Black" were published in *Inlandia: A Literary Journey Volume 14.* The Poetic Genius hopes that his poetry will honor his people and inspire many, including his singer/songwriter daughter, Layla. Currently, he attends monthly open mics with Slam Connection and works with their team to build a community of poetry and outreach in Williamsburg, Virginia.

Benjamin S. Grossberg

Benjamin S. Grossberg's books of poetry include *My Husband Would* (University of Tampa, 2020), winner of the 2021 Connecticut Book Award, and *Sweet Core Orchard* (University of Tampa, 2009), winner of a Lambda Literary Award. He also wrote the novel, *The Spring Before Obergefell* (University of Nebraska Press, 2024), winner of the 2023 AWP Award Series James Alan McPherson Prize. He teaches at the University of Hartford.

Mark Andrew Heathcote

Mark Andrew Heathcote is an adult learning difficulties support worker. He has poems published in journals, magazines, and anthologies online and in print. He resides in the UK and is from Manchester. Mark is the author of *In Perpetuity* and *Back on Earth*, two books of poems published by Creative Talents Unleashed.

Erin Jamieson

Erin Jamieson (she/her) holds an MFA in Creative Writing from Miami University. Her writing has been published in over eighty literary magazines, including two Pushcart Prize nominations. She is the author of a poetry collection, *Clothesline*, (NiftyLit, Feb 2023). Her latest poetry chapbook, *Fairytales*, was published by Bottlecap

Press. Her debut novel, *Sky of Ashes, Land of Dreams*, came out November 2023. Twitter: @erin_simmer

---

Natalie Kimbell

Natalie Kimbell grew up in Sequatchie County, Tennessee. She has spent forty years teaching English and theater arts there. She is a mother, grandmother and lover of all things that sparkle. Her work appears in *Pine Mountain Sand and Gravel*, *Mildred Haun Review*, *Anthology of Appalachian Writers*, *Artemis*, *Tennessee Voices*, and *23 Tales: Appalachian Ghost Stories, Legends and Other Mysteries*. Her first poetry chapbook, *On Phillips Creek*, will be published by Finishing Line Press in 2024.

Payton Kohan

Payton Kohan is a writer, bookworm, and fairy tale enthusiast. She holds a BA in English from Thomas Edison State University. Her short story, "The Final Key," was published in Ocean County College's 2021 *Seascape* magazine and awarded first prize. She lives in New Jersey with her parents, sister, and two cats.

D.L. Lang

D.L. Lang served as Poet Laureate of Vallejo, California. She is published in over 60 anthologies worldwide. She is a co-founder of Vallejo Poetry Society and a member of the Revolutionary Poets Brigade. She was the editor of *Verses, Voices, & Visions of Vallejo*. She has performed her poetry hundreds of times at festivals, demonstrations, and literary events across California. Her poems have been transformed into songs, used as liturgy, and to advocate for a better world. Find her online at <u>poetryebook.com</u>

Bianca Lopez

The greatest temptation a writer must face is the resistance to find comfort in being defined. To be keen on tirelessly focusing on life all around, to stay true to the very essence of human experiences, break barriers, cross boundaries while retaining humanity is what, author, Bianca Lopez seeks through her writing.

Writing is rebellion. To become a trailblazer of expression in pursuit of universal truth, while embracing rebellion; rebellion against stereotypes, non-conformity, limited thinking, narrow mindedness and above all freedom of expression is what motivates Bianca.

After having extensively traveled to over 43 countries, she proudly amassed a plethora of experiences and wealth of knowledge to be showcased in her body of works. Bianca's main source of influence comes from the many years of theatrical studies in different programs such as with Jeremy Geidt at Harvard University's Tony Award-winning American Repertory Theatre, undergraduate studies at Columbia University Theatre, method acting at The Lee Strasberg Theatre and Film Institute in New York City, and London Academy of Music and Dramatic Art's Shakespeare Intensive.

Bianca holds a Bachelor of Fine Arts in Film/Television Production as a Magna Cum Laude at New York University's Tisch School of the Arts. She was recently accepted into the extremely competitive Yale Writers' Workshop. Bianca now looks forward to her next venture with New Perspective's Theatre Company as a dramaturg and director for this year's upcoming Women's Work Lab.

Nancy Lubarsky

Nancy Lubarsky, a retired school superintendent, has been published in various journals including *Exit 13, Lips, Tiferet, Stillwater Review,* and *Paterson Literary Review*. She's authored two books: *Tattoos* (Finishing Line) and *The Only Proof* (Kelsay). Her manuscript, *Truth to the Rumors,* was one of five finalist for the 2023 Laura Boss Narrative Poetry Award—anticipated publishing date, Fall, 2023, by Kelsay Press.

Fhen M.

The vernacular poem "Uyasan" ("Toy" in English") written by Fhen M. was published in a collection of literary works entitled *Pinili: 15 Years of Lamiraw*. His English verses "Lighthouse," "Seaport," "Barbeque Stalls along Boulevard," and "Tetrapod" appeared in *Poetica* anthology series published by Clarendon House. Fhen M. was a writing fellow at the Lamiraw Creative Writing Workshop. He was one of the winners of the 1st Chito Roño Literary Awards in the poetry category. Also, he was a daily winner of a radio poetry contest sponsored by a radio station based in Eastern Visayas.

J.S. Mannino

J.S. Mannino is a Florida poet who once had a poem turned into a song and performed for his school. He's been chasing the breakout success of "Roller Skates" ever since. In complement to his passion for writing, he loves running, climbing, and cooking.

Bruce McRae

Bruce McRae, a Canadian musician, is a multiple Pushcart nominee with poems published in hundreds of magazines such as *Poetry, Rattle,* and the *North American Review*. The winner of the 2020 Libretto prize and author of four poetry collections and seven chapbooks, his poems have been broadcast and performed globally.

Norman Minnick

Norman Minnick is the author of three collections of poetry and editor of several anthologies. Most recently, he is the editor of *The Lost Etheridge: Uncollected Poems of Etheridge Knight*. Visit www. buzzminnick.com for more information.

Abigail Ottley

Abigail Ottley's poetry and short fiction have been widely published over ten years, most recently in *Atrium, The Phare,* and *Ink, Sweat & Tears*. She is a regular contributor to anthologies including *Invisible Borders: New Women's Writing From Cornwall, Morvoren: the poetry of sea-swimming,* and *Unbridled: Women's Poetry*. In May this year, two pamphlets were placed third and Highly Commended in the Frosted Fire Pamphlet Award and, in June, she won the Wildfire Flash Fiction Competition. In October she was long-listed for the Ink of Ages historical short fiction award.

Julia M. Paul

Julia M. Paul is author of two full-length collections, *Shook and Table with Burning Candle* (forthcoming in 2024) and a chapbook, *Staring Down the Tracks*. Her poem "Dear Coroner, How Could You Know," first published in *Here*, appears in the *2023 Pushcart Prize XLVII: Best of the Small Presses* anthology. She serves as president of the Riverwood Poetry Series, a long-running reading series in Hartford, Connecticut, and is an elder law attorney in Manchester, Connecticut.

Faith Paulsen

Faith Paulsen's work appears or is upcoming in *Scientific American, Poetry Breakfast, Milk art journal, Philadelphia Stories, Book of Matches, One Art, Panoply, Thimble, Evansville Review* and *Mantis*. The author of three chapbooks and mother of three sons, her day job is in insurance.

https://www.faithpaulsenpoet.com/

Lois Perch Villemaire

Lois Perch Villemaire is the author of *My Eight Greats*, a family history in poetry and prose published in 2023. Her work has appeared in such places as *Blue Mountain Review, Ekphrastic Review, One Art: A Journal of Poetry, Pen In Hand and* Topical Poetry. Anthologies, including *I Am My Father's Daughter* and *Truth Serum Press - Lifespan Series*, have published her memoir and poetry. Originally from the Philadelphia area, Lois lives in Annapolis, MD, where she enjoys yoga, researching family connections, fun photography, and doting over her African violets.

Thomas Rions-Maehren

Thomas Rions-Maehren is a bilingual poet, novelist, and chemist who explores the dark places of human experience with humor, science, and (at times) tranquility and wisdom. His scientific research has been published in *ACS Nano*, and examples of his Spanish-language prose can be found in his published short stories and in his novel *En las Manos de Satanás* (Ápeiron Ediciones, 2022). More of his poetry in both languages can be found in a number of journals, such as *The Elevation* and *Pensive*, at his blog (tommaehrenpoetry.blogspot.com), and at his website (thomasrionsmaehren.com). He is on Twitter and Instagram @MaehrenTom.

Stephanie Robertazzi

Born and raised in New Jersey, Stephanie Robertazzi holds a MA in Educational Leadership from Kean University and a BA in English and Secondary Education from Georgian Court University. When Stephanie isn't teaching high school English, you may find her spending time with her husband or making memories with her two sons, family, and friends, and her lemon beagle, Holly.

Brittany Rostron and Willian John Rostron

William John Rostron has published four novels set in the world of 1960s New York culture and music. An integral plot theme of these novels involves a struggling group of musicians who create original songs that are the key to their success. In his quest to give lyrics to these fictional songs, he came upon a poem his daughter, Brittany Rostron, wrote a quarter of a century ago. Changing the title and some the lyrics, it became "Thief of My Forever." Brittany, in turn, took a chapter of her father's first book, *Band in the Wind*, and created the script for a film short titled, *Pretty Flamingo*. The script received critical acclaim from ten Hollywood and New York Festivals. A proof-of-concept film was created in 2023 and won the New York Long Island Film Festival in its category. Key to this success was the inclusion of "Thief" as it was reworked by father and daughter to fit the film script. It is sung by the main character Johnny and played by studio musicians during the credits. To see the film *Pretty Flamingo* (8 minutes) and hear the song "Thief," go to www.PrettyFlamingoFilm.com. To learn more about William John Rostron, go to www.WilliamJohnRostron.com. To learn more about Brittany Rostron and her twenty-year career in movies, go to www.Femaleaces.org or www.PrettyFlamingoFilm.com.

Andy Stephen

Andy Stephen is a music teacher located in coastal New Jersey. He has been writing poetry for many years and is thrilled to have his first publication.

JC Sulzenko

Canadian JC Sulzenko's poetry appeared in anthologies and journals in print and online, either under her name or as A. Garnett Weiss. Her cento won the 2023 Wind & Water Writing Contest. Aeolus House published *Bricolage, A Gathering of Centos*, a finalist for the Canadian Authors Association's 2022 Fred Kerner Book Award. Point Petre Publishing released *South Shore Suite...POEMS* in 2017. JC's publications for children and families include a play on dementia. She has offered workshops for the Ottawa International Writers Festival, County Arts, school boards, municipal libraries, and Alzheimer societies. A full member of the League of Canadian Poets, she selects for <u>bywords.ca</u> and serves on the Board of the Ontario Poetry Society. <u>www.jcsulzenko.com.</u>

Jelena Tutnjevic

Jelena Tutnjevic is an aspiring writer currently living in Ottawa, Canada. She was born in Sarajevo, Bosnia, and Herzegovina and immigrated to Canada in 1995 following the civil war breaking out in her country. She settled in Ottawa where she earned a Bachelor and Masters Degree in English Literature. While studying, she published several articles in a Toronto based magazine called *Man and Thought*, and she was also one of the honorary winners in the Broken English short story competition in Ottawa. Her work life in Canada began with the Great Canadian Theatre Company, and then she moved on to work in a non-profit organization advocating for rights of Aboriginal women before starting her current career as a public servant. Writing was part of her life as long as she remembers, and writing poetry is her greatest passion.

Henry Vinicio Valerio Madriz

Born in Atenas, Costa Rica, 1969, Henry Vinicio Valerio Madriz graduated in English Teaching and Linguistics & Literature. Photography lover. He's published "Strange Fate", Darkness Falls, "Loving Shadows", "Dear You," "My Superheroes", KAPOW!, The Red Penguin, USA; "Running", Strangest Fiction Volume One, USA; "The Cyrenian," Otherwise Engaged Literature and Arts Journal Volume 11, USA; "My Love's Gone On A Train" and "Treasure," Younker! The Flight Of Youthful Temptations, India; and "Green Mirrors," All Your Stories, December 2023, UK. He got shortlisted with his poem "Soldiers' Death Sentence" in Voice of Peace: 1st

Intercontinental Poetry And Short Story Anthology 2021, The League of Poets.

Barry Vitcov

Barry Vitcov lives in Ashland, Oregon, with his wife and an exceptionally brilliant standard poodle. He has had two books published by Finishing Line Press, a collection of poetry, *Where I Live Some of the Time* in February 2021 and a collection of short stories, *The Wilbur Stories & More* in June 2022. FLP will be publishing a chapbook collection of poems, *Structures,* in May 2024 and a novella, *The Boy with Six Fingers*, in June 2025.

Suellen Wedmore

Suellen Wedmore, Poet Laureate emerita for the seaside town of Rockport, Massachusetts, and an involved member of the Cape Ann Massachusetts community, with its deep-rooted fishing heritage, wrote "A Fisherman's Wife Greets the Dawn Alone" in sympathy with the courageous women and men whose lives have been and continue to be interwoven with the sea. Four of her published poems have been nominated for a Pushcart Prize, and her full-length book, *A Fixed White Light*, which features the voices of six nineteenth-century courageous women lighthouse keepers, was recently published by Down East Books.

Scott Wiggerman

A member of the Texas Institute of Letters, Albuquerque poet Scott Wiggerman is the author of three books of poetry, *Leaf and Beak:*

Sonnets, Presence, and *Vegetables and Other Relationships*; and the editor of several volumes, including *Wingbeats I & II: Exercises & Practice in Poetry,* and the brand-new anthology *Unknotting the Line: The Poetry in Prose.* In recent years, haiku and art have become more central to his work as an artist of both the page and canvas.

Andrena Zawinski

Andrena Zawinski is the author of four full-length collections of poetry, several smaller volumes, and a book of flash fiction. Her latest collection of poetry is *Born Under the Influence* and her flash fiction is *Plumes & Other Flights of Fancy.* She lives in the San Francisco Bay Area.

ABOUT THE EDITOR

Photo by Tim of EVNFLO Photography

Jill Ocone has been a high school communications/journalism and English teacher since 2001 and a writer/editor for *Jersey Shore Magazine/Jersey Shore Publications* since 2014. Her debut novel, *Enduring the Waves*, was traditionally published in November 2023 by The Wild Rose Press. Her work has also been published in *Beach Badge Issue 4* (Eight Stone Press), Read Furiously's anthology *Stay Salty: Life in the Garden State; The Winward Review* (2019 issue), Exeter Publishing's *From the Soil* hometown anthology; Red Penguin Books'

Where Flowers Bloom, the leaves fall and *'Tis the Season: Poems for Your Holiday Spirit;* and *American Writers Review-A Literary Journal* (2022, 2020 and 2019 volumes), among others. She is an alumnus of the Yale Writing Workshop. She enjoys making memories with her nieces and nephews, yoga, seeing new places, laughing with her family and friends, and sharing her Jersey Shore home with her husband. Visit Jill online at www.jillocone.com.

Milton Keynes UK
Ingram Content Group UK Ltd.
UKHW011133220424
441551UK00006B/506